FOUR-TASTIC FAMILY NIGHTS

FOUR ACTION-PACKED FAMILY DEVOTIONS EACH MONTH

The Adventures of
Pookie

REBECCA YEE

TABLE OF CONTENTS

INTRODUCTION

Welcome to a year of growing closer to God together!

Families are busy, life moves fast, and everyone has different schedules. But when you take just a little time each week to pause, listen, and learn from God's Word as a family, something amazing happens: faith grows, hearts bond, and your home becomes a place where God's love shines every day.

This devotional is designed to help your family build a rhythm of faith that is **simple, fun, and meaningful**. You don't have to be perfect at it. Just show up, open your hearts, and trust that God is at work in your home this year!

HOW TO USE THIS DEVOTIONAL AS A FAMILY

Each month has a theme that helps your family focus on one big truth from Scripture. Then each week includes:

- » **Verse of the Week** — A key Bible verse to read together and remember.
- » **Object Lesson** — A practical connection that brings Scripture to life.
- » **Devotional Thought** — A simple, encouraging message that helps kids understand what God's Word means for their everyday lives.
- » **Family Discussion Questions** — Celebrate what everyone is learning and help kids grow in confidence talking about faith.
- » **Prayer** — A moment to talk to God together.
- » **Family Challenge of the Week** — A real-world way to live out the devotion as a family.

You can do one devotional each week, whichever day works best. There's no "right way" or "wrong way" to use this book. The goal is to **spend time with God and with each other**.

TIPS FOR FAMILY FAITH TIME

Here are a few ideas to help your time together feel peaceful and purposeful:

- ✓ Set aside a specific day or time (like Sunday nights or Saturday mornings).
- ✓ Keep distractions away—everyone's attention matters.
- ✓ Let kids participate! Take turns reading verses or answering questions.
- ✓ Celebrate each person's thoughts and ideas, no answer is too small.
- ✓ Keep it positive. God loves when His children learn and grow.
- ✓ End with a hug, a high five, or a family cheer!

A short moment of faith each week can make a big difference in everyone's life.

MEMORY VERSES & SCRIPTURE HABITS

God's Word gives us strength, comfort, and guidance. Memorizing Scripture helps kids, and adults, carry God's truth with them everywhere they go.

Here are some simple ideas for building Scripture habits:

- **Write the Verse** — Put the week's verse on the fridge, bathroom mirror, or by the front door. Refresh it each week!
- **Make It a Song** — Kids remember things better when they sing them! Make up a tune, rap it, or clap along.
- **Break It into Pieces** — Learn a few words each day and celebrate when the whole verse is memorized.
- **Say It Together** — At meals, bedtimes, or car rides, repeat the verse as a family.
- **Verse Challenge** — Record yourselves saying the verse at the end of the week and celebrate progress.

Remember—memorizing Scripture isn't about perfection, it's about *tucking God's truth into our hearts*.

FINAL THOUGHT BEFORE YOU BEGIN

This year, your family is going to explore God's love, hope, strength, joy, and purpose. You will learn more about Jesus and discover the amazing ways He wants to work through your family every day.

Invite God into every moment, and get ready for a powerful year of faith and fun!

Let's begin!

JANUARY

NEW BEGINNINGS

Devotional 1
GOD MAKES ALL THINGS NEW

Verse of the Week

Therefore, if anyone is in Christ, the new creation has come: The old has gone, the new is here!
-2 Corinthians 5:17(NIV)

Object Lesson

Take a sheet of paper and crumple it into a tight ball. Then try to smooth it out again. Even though you flatten it, the wrinkles remain. Now take a *fresh, clean sheet* and hold it up. It has no creases, completely new. That's what Jesus does with our hearts. He doesn't just smooth out the old; He gives us a brand-new start.

Devotional

A new year always feels like a fresh beginning. We buy new calendars, set new goals, and imagine how things might be different. But the "newness" that God gives us goes far deeper than turning a page on the calendar. According to today's verse, anyone who belongs to Jesus becomes a new creation. That means God doesn't just fix up the old parts of us, He transforms us from the inside out.

Sometimes we remember our mistakes from the past year: the times we got angry, disobeyed, or felt like we weren't enough. But Jesus promises a clean slate. When we trust Him, He wipes away the "wrinkles" of our sin and gives us His forgiveness, strength, and hope. We can move forward without carrying old guilt or shame.

This week, every time you see something new—new clothes, a new notebook, a new day—let it remind you that **Jesus makes your heart new too**. And when God starts something new in us, He promises to help us grow into who He created us to be.

Family Discussion Questions

1. What is something from last year that you're glad God forgives?
2. What does becoming a "new creation" mean to you?
3. What is one area where you want God to help you grow this year?

Prayer

Dear Jesus, thank You for making us new. Thank You for forgiving our mistakes and giving us a fresh start. Help us walk into this new year with hearts open to Your love and Your plans. Make us more like You every day. Amen.

Family Challenge of the Week

Create a "New Beginnings List."

Each family member writes down one thing they want God to make new in their life this year. Hang the list somewhere visible and pray over it this week.

Devotional 2
STARTING THE YEAR WITH PURPOSE

Verse of the Week

Commit to the Lord whatever you do, and he will establish your plans. -Proverbs 16:3(NIV)

Object Lesson

Set a puzzle box on the table. If you try to build the puzzle without looking at the picture on the front, the pieces may fit together, but it's so much harder. But when you look at the picture, the whole puzzle makes sense. Committing your plans to God is like looking at the picture before you begin. It gives direction and purpose.

Devotional

At the start of the year, many people make resolutions or goals. Some want to exercise more, read more, or try something new. These are good things, but God invites us to do something even greater: **give our plans to Him first**. Proverbs 16:3 tells us that when we commit what we do to the Lord, He helps shape and guide the path ahead.

That doesn't mean everything will be perfect or easy. It means God becomes the One who directs our steps, opens the right doors, and gives wisdom when we feel unsure. When we invite Him into our decisions, big or small, we are choosing to live with purpose instead of guessing our way through life like a puzzle without the picture.

This year, we can ask God to guide our family's choices, time, and priorities. We can pray about our schedules, friendships, schoolwork, and dreams. When God is at the center, the pieces of our lives start fitting together in ways that bring peace, joy, and direction.

Family Discussion Questions

1. What are some goals you have for this year?
2. Why do you think it's important to commit our plans to God first?
3. What is one thing our family can pray about as we make decisions this year?

Prayer

Lord, we give You our plans, our choices, and our dreams. Help us listen to Your guidance and follow Your direction. Make our steps firm and purposeful as we walk with You this year. Amen.

Family Challenge of the Week

Make a Family Vision Board.

Cut out pictures or draw goals for the year. Pray over the board and ask God to lead your family's plans.

Devotional 3
LEAVING WORRIES BEHIND

Verse of the Week

Do not be anxious about anything, but in every situation, by prayer and petition, with thanksgiving, present your requests to God. And the peace of God, which transcends all understanding, will guard your hearts and your minds in Christ Jesus. -Philippians 4:6–7(NIV)

Object Lesson

Give each person a balloon. Ask them to blow it up while thinking of something that worries them. When everyone is ready, release the balloons and watch them fly around the room. Just like that balloon, God invites us to *let go* of our worries instead of holding them tightly inside.

Devotional

Worries often grow when we carry them alone. We think about school, work, friendships, money, health, or things that might happen. But God doesn't want us to live weighed down by fear or stress. Philippians 4:6–7 gives us a gentle but powerful instruction: *Don't be anxious, pray instead*. When we talk to God about what we're scared of, confused about, or stressed over, He replaces our anxiety with His incredible peace.

This peace isn't like the calm we feel when everything in life is perfect. God's peace is stronger. It guards our hearts and minds, even when things are uncertain. It reminds us that

God is bigger than our worries, closer than our fears, and more faithful than we could imagine.

Letting go of worry doesn't mean ignoring our problems. It means trusting that we don't face them alone. This week, as you feel worry rising up, pause and whisper a simple prayer: *"Jesus, take this."* He hears every worry-filled whisper and responds with His comfort.

Family Discussion Questions

1. What is something you tend to worry about?
2. How does praying change the way we feel about our worries?
3. What can our family do this week to give our worries to God?

Prayer

Jesus, thank You for caring about our worries—even the small ones. Help us remember to bring everything to You in prayer. Fill our hearts and minds with Your peace this week. Amen.

Family Challenge of the Week

Create a "Worry Box."

Write your worries on small slips of paper and place them in the box. Pray as a family, asking God to take each worry and replace it with His peace.

Devotional 4
TRUSTING GOD WITH THE FUTURE

Verse of the Week

Trust in the Lord with all your heart and lean not on your own understanding; in all your ways submit to him, and he will make your paths straight. -Proverbs 3:5–6(NIV)

Object Lesson

Blindfold one family member and create a simple obstacle course in the living room. Another family member guides the blindfolded person with verbal instructions. The blindfolded person must trust the guide completely, just like we trust God to lead us even when we can't see what comes next.

Devotional

The future is full of unknowns. We don't know what challenges, blessings, surprises, or changes are coming. But God does. Proverbs 3:5–6 tells us to trust Him with our whole heart, not just the parts that feel easy. Trusting God means believing that His way is best, even when we can't see the full picture.

Sometimes the path ahead feels confusing or scary. We want answers right now. But God invites us to take one step at a time, following His guidance through prayer, His Word, and wise voices in our lives. When we lean on Him instead of our own understanding, He promises to "make our paths straight," meaning He leads us in the direction that is good, right, and full of purpose.

This year, instead of trying to control everything, we can choose to trust God with what's ahead, our school year, relationships, big decisions, and everyday moments. He has never failed His people, and He won't start now.

Family Discussion Questions

1. What future situation are you nervous or excited about?
2. What does it look like to trust God with your whole heart?
3. How can our family encourage each other to follow God's guidance this year?

Prayer

Father, we choose to trust You with everything ahead of us. Lead our steps, guide our decisions, and remind us that You are in control. Help us follow Your path with courage and faith. Amen.

Family Challenge of the Week

Create a "Faith Step" Jar.

Each person writes one thing they want to trust God with in the future. Place the notes in a jar and pray over them daily this week, asking God to lead your family's steps.

FEBRUARY

LOVE LIKE JESUS

Devotional 1
GOD'S UNCONDITIONAL LOVE

Verse of the Week

For God so loved the world that he gave his one and only Son, that whoever believes in him shall not perish but have eternal life. -John 3:16(NIV)

Object Lesson

Hold up a mirror. Ask everyone what they see. Then say, "God loves that person more than you can imagine." No matter how we look, feel, or act on our worst day, God's love never changes. The mirror reminds us that *God's love is personal, He loves YOU*.

Devotional

John 3:16 is one of the most famous verses in the Bible, and for a good reason. It tells the greatest love story ever told. God didn't just talk about love; He showed it in the most powerful way possible. He gave His Son, Jesus, so we could be forgiven, saved, and brought close to Him. This love wasn't earned. We didn't work hard enough or behave well enough to deserve it. God loved us *first*, completely and unconditionally.

That means God's love doesn't disappear when we make mistakes. It doesn't shrink when we have a bad attitude. It doesn't fade when we feel unworthy. His love remains steady, strong, and overflowing, because it's rooted in who **He** is, not who **we** are.

When we truly understand God's love, it changes us. It gives us confidence when we feel afraid, comfort when we feel alone, and hope when life is hard. Let this verse remind your family that God's love is the foundation of everything we believe. You are fully known, fully loved, and fully welcomed into His heart.

Family Discussion Questions

1. What does "unconditional love" mean to you?
2. How does knowing God loves you change the way you see yourself?
3. How can we remind ourselves of God's love this week?

Prayer

Father, thank You for loving us more than we can understand. Help us rest in Your love and remember that nothing can separate us from it. Let Your love fill our hearts and guide our lives. Amen.

Family Challenge of the Week

Make Heart Notes.

Write encouraging "God loves you!" notes and hide them around the house for each other to find throughout the week.

Devotional 2
LOVING OUR FAMILY WELL

Verse of the Week

Dear children, let us not love with words or speech but with actions and in truth. -1 John 3:18(NIV)

Object Lesson

Place a flashlight on the table and switch it off. Say, "This flashlight *says* it's a light, but without the battery, it doesn't actually shine." Our words are like the outside of the flashlight, but our actions are the battery. Without actions, love can't shine.

Devotional

It's easy to say, "*I love you*," but God calls us to show love in the everyday moments of family life. Sometimes that means helping without being asked, speaking kindly when we're frustrated, or choosing patience over arguing. Love is more than a feeling, it's a choice we make again and again.

In families, we see the real test of love. We see each other tired, stressed, or upset. But this gives us a beautiful opportunity: we get to practice real, Christ-like love right at home. When we choose to love each other through our actions, we reflect Jesus. We show humility, kindness, and compassion, not because we always feel like it, but because Jesus first loved us.

This week is an opportunity for your family to become "love

in action." Ask God to help you see the small moments where love is needed—a chore nobody wants to do, a sibling who needs encouragement, a parent who needs support, a moment to be gentle instead of irritated. Every action of love shines His light.

Family Discussion Questions

1. What are some ways we can show love at home this week?
2. Why are actions sometimes more powerful than words?
3. Who in our family could use extra love or encouragement right now?

Prayer

Jesus, help us love our family the way You love us—with patience, kindness, and compassion. Show us where we can serve and encourage each other through our actions. Amen.

Family Challenge of the Week

Secret Service Week.

Each family member becomes a "secret helper," doing anonymous acts of kindness for others in the home.

Devotional 3
KINDNESS IN ACTION

Verse of the Week

Be kind and compassionate to one another, forgiving each
other, just as in Christ God forgave you.
-Ephesians 4:32(NIV)

Object Lesson

Give each person two cups, one empty, one filled with
water. The water represents kindness. When someone
pours kindness into our lives, we "overflow." Let each
person pour a little water into someone else's cup to show
how kindness spreads from person to person.

Devotional

Kindness seems small, but it has incredible power. A kind
word can lift someone's spirit. A gentle response can stop
an argument. A forgiving heart can heal a relationship.
Today's verse reminds us that kindness isn't just something
we do when it's easy, *it's part of living like Jesus*.

When Jesus walked on earth, He noticed the people
everyone else ignored. He stopped to help the hurting,
welcomed the lonely, and forgave those who failed Him.
His kindness wasn't random; it was intentional. In the same
way, we have opportunities every day to show compassion:
at school, at home, online, and wherever we go.

Sometimes kindness is simple, like sharing or holding the

door. Other times it's hard, like forgiving someone who hurt us. But God gives us the strength to show kindness because *He* has shown so much kindness to us.

This week, think of kindness as a ripple. One small act can create waves that touch more people than you realize.

Family Discussion Questions

1. What is one small act of kindness you can do for someone this week?
2. Why is forgiveness an important part of kindness?
3. Who in your world (school, family, neighborhood) needs compassion right now?

Prayer

Lord, thank You for showing kindness and compassion to us every day. Help us spread kindness wherever we go. Fill our hearts with Your love so we can forgive and care for others. Amen.

Family Challenge of the Week

Kindness Bingo.

Create a simple 9–12 square bingo board with acts of kindness. Try to complete a "kindness row" as a family by the end of the week.

(You can also download a Kindness Bingo card from our website AdventuresOfPookie.com)

Devotional 4
LOVING OTHERS WHO ARE DIFFERENT

Verse of the Week

Therefore let us stop passing judgment on one another. Instead, make up your mind not to put any stumbling block or obstacle in the way of a brother or sister.
-Romans 14:13(NIV)

Object Lesson

Have each family member find two socks that look completely different (different colors, patterns, or lengths). Put them on together. At first, they may look odd or mismatched. But then ask: *Do they still keep your feet warm? Can you still walk?* Even though the socks don't match, they both have value and purpose.

Devotional

God created every person uniquely. We have different personalities, talents, backgrounds, and opinions. Sometimes, those differences can make us uncomfortable or unsure how to act. But Romans 14:13 reminds us that instead of judging or looking down on others, we should make it *easier* for them to know and experience God's love.

That means we don't let differences become obstacles. Instead, we choose kindness, patience, and understanding. Loving others who are different might look like sitting with the new kid at school, including someone who feels left out, or being gentle with someone whose personality is different from ours.

Jesus did this beautifully. He welcomed people from every walk of life—rich, poor, healthy, sick, joyful, broken, old, young. He didn't push people away because they were different. He drew them close. When we love others the way Jesus did, we show the world what God's heart looks like.

Family Discussion Questions

1. Why is it sometimes hard to love people who are different from us?
2. What is one way we can remove obstacles for someone this week?
3. Who in your school or community might need extra love or acceptance?

Prayer

God, thank You for making every person unique. Help us love people who are different from us with patience, kindness, and a welcoming heart. Show us how to remove obstacles and be a light for others. Amen.

Family Challenge of the Week

"Include Someone New" Challenge.

Each family member chooses one person this week to include, encourage, or show kindness to.

MARCH

GROWING IN FAITH

Devotional 1
PLANTING SEEDS OF FAITH

Verse of the Week

The seed is the word of God... But the seed on good soil stands for those with a noble and good heart, who hear the word, retain it, and by persevering produce a crop.
-Luke 8:11 & 15(NIV)

Object Lesson

Give each family member a few seeds and a cup of soil. Let everyone plant their seed. Explain that the seed will grow only when given good soil, water, and sunlight, just like faith grows when we hear God's Word, hold onto it, and put it into practice.

Devotional

Jesus often used gardening to teach spiritual truths. In today's verses, He explains that God's Word is like a seed planted in our hearts. But for seeds to grow, the soil has to be ready. Hard or crowded soil doesn't help anything grow. But good soil, soft, open, and cared for, produces something strong, healthy, and fruitful.

Our hearts work the same way. When we hear God's Word but don't think about it or apply it, it doesn't grow. But when we listen, reflect, ask questions, and try to live out what God says, faith begins to take root. Over time, it grows into actions, attitudes, and choices that honor God.

Just like seeds don't sprout overnight, faith takes time. We keep reading the Bible, praying, and trusting God, and He helps us grow stronger every day. This month is a reminder that faith isn't something we just "have", it's something we nurture.

Family Discussion Questions

1. What helps faith grow in your heart?
2. What are some "weeds" (distractions or habits) that make it harder to grow in faith?
3. How can we plant "good seeds" this week?

Prayer

Lord, plant Your Word deep in our hearts. Help us be good soil—ready, open, and eager to grow. Teach us to listen, learn, and follow You every day. Amen.

Family Challenge of the Week

Plant a real seed or small plant together.

Check on it throughout the week, using it as a reminder that faith grows when we care for it.

Devotional 2
LISTENING TO GOD

Verse of the Week

My sheep listen to my voice; I know them, and they follow me. -John 10:27(NIV)

Object Lesson

Play a "voice recognition" game. Have everyone close their eyes. One person makes a sound or says a word, and everyone else guesses who it was. Explain that just like we learn the voices of people we love, we can learn to recognize God's voice too.

Devotional

Jesus calls Himself our Shepherd, and we are His sheep. Sheep aren't the fastest or the strongest animals, but what makes them safe is their ability to recognize and follow their shepherd's voice. They learn it by staying close, listening, and trusting. Jesus wants us to have that same kind of relationship with Him.

But how do we "hear" God's voice? God speaks through His Word, through the Holy Spirit's nudges in our hearts, through wise people, and sometimes through quiet moments in prayer. The more time we spend with Him, the easier it is to recognize when He is guiding us, warning us, or comforting us.

In a world filled with noise, screens, busy schedules,

opinions, distractions, it can be hard to slow down enough to listen. But listening to God is part of growing in faith. When we listen, we learn His heart. When we follow, we walk in His peace and protection.

Family Discussion Questions

1. What are some ways God speaks to us today?
2. What makes it hard to hear God's voice sometimes?
3. How can we make quiet space to listen to Him this week?

Prayer

Jesus, thank You for being our Shepherd. Help us learn Your voice. Quiet the distractions around us and guide us into Your truth. Help us follow You wherever You lead. Amen.

Family Challenge of the Week

Take a 5-minute family "quiet time."

Sit together with no screens, no talking—just silence. Afterward, share anything God brought to your heart.

Devotional 3
BUILDING GOOD HABITS

Verse of the Week

Do not conform to the pattern of this world, but be transformed by the renewing of your mind. Then you will be able to test and approve what God's will is—his good, pleasing and perfect will. -Romans 12:2(NIV)

Object Lesson

Set out two jars: one labeled GOOD HABITS, one labeled BAD HABITS. Give each person small stones or pom-poms. Ask them to drop items into whichever jar fits: prayer, complaining, kindness, rushing, reading the Bible, arguing, serving others, etc. Explain that the habits we choose shape who we become.

Devotional

Every day, we make choices that become habits. Some habits help us grow. Like being thankful, reading the Bible, praying, being responsible, or speaking kindly. Other habits hold us back or pull us away from God's best. God doesn't want us to simply copy the world around us. Instead, He invites us to be transformed, to think differently, act differently, and grow to look more like Jesus.

We can't change all our habits overnight, and God doesn't expect us to be perfect. But He does ask us to take small, consistent steps. When we fill our minds with God's truth instead of negativity or distraction, it changes the way we live. When we practice good habits, our faith grows stronger.

This week's verse reminds us that real transformation happens from the inside out. God renews our minds, giving us wisdom, courage, and clarity. And as our minds change, our choices begin to change too. One good habit at a time, God is helping us grow.

Family Discussion Questions

1. What is one habit you want to build this month?
2. What is one habit you want to break or change?
3. How can our family encourage each other in our habits?

Prayer

God, help us build habits that honor You. Renew our minds with Your truth and help us choose actions that draw us closer to You every day. Give us strength to grow, learn, and change. Amen.

Family Challenge of the Week

Start one new faith habit together.

Choose a simple habit, like praying before school, reading a verse at dinner, or saying one kind word daily, and practice it all week.

Devotional 4
WHEN FAITH FEELS SMALL

Verse of the Week

He replied, "Because you have so little faith. Truly I tell you, if you have faith as small as a mustard seed, you can say to this mountain, 'Move from here to there,' and it will move. Nothing will be impossible for you. -Matthew 17:20(NIV)

Object Lesson

Show a mustard seed (or a picture of one). It's tiny, almost too small to hold. Then show a photo of the full-grown plant. Explain that Jesus says even the smallest faith can grow into something strong and powerful.

Devotional

Sometimes faith feels easy, like when prayers are answered quickly or everything is going well. But other times, faith feels small. Maybe we have doubts. Maybe we're scared. Maybe life is confusing. Jesus knew we would face moments like this, and that's why He used the mustard seed as an example.

A mustard seed is tiny, but when planted, it becomes one of the largest garden plants. Jesus' message is simple: It's not the size of your faith that matters, it's the power of the One you're trusting. Even small faith, when placed in a big God, can do amazing things.

If you feel unsure or weak, that doesn't disqualify you. It

means you're human and you're invited to rely on God even more. He can grow your faith one step at a time. Small prayers matter. Small acts of obedience matter. Small steps of trust matter. Over time, they lead to strong, steady faith.

Family Discussion Questions

1. When does your faith feel small?
2. What is one small step of faith you can take this week?
3. How has God helped your faith grow in the past?

Prayer

Lord, thank You that even small faith matters to You. Take our tiny seeds of faith and help them grow. Give us courage to trust You even when things feel uncertain or scary.
Amen.

Family Challenge of the Week

Do one "mustard seed step."

Choose one small but meaningful step of faith, praying for someone, forgiving someone, trying something new, or trusting God with something hard.

APRIL

HOPE & REDEMPTION

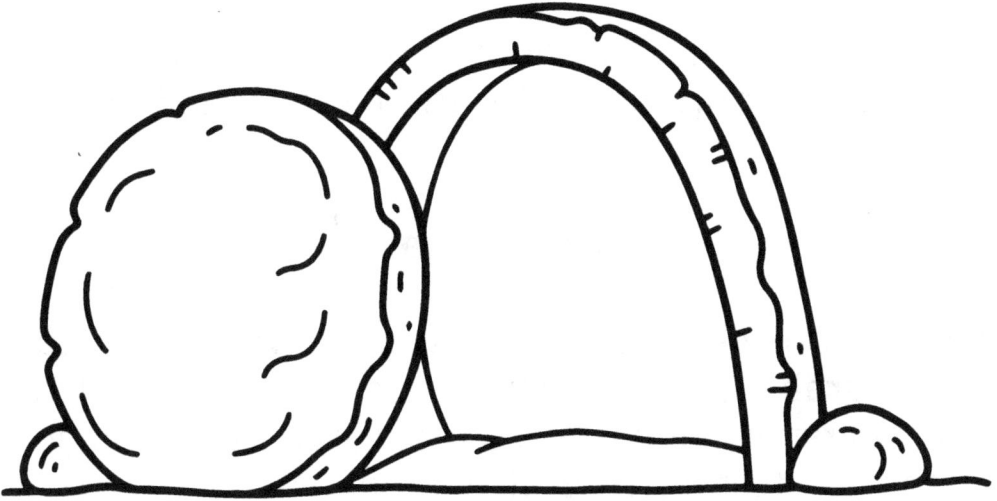

Devotional 1
WHY JESUS CAME

Verse of the Week

For God so loved the world that he gave his one and only Son, that whoever believes in him shall not perish but have eternal life. For God did not send his Son into the world to condemn the world, but to save the world through him.
-John 3:16-17(NIV)

Object Lesson

Hold up a first aid kit. Talk about how it's used to help people who are hurt, not to tell them they shouldn't have gotten hurt.

Devotional

When someone gets hurt, the first thing we do is try to help them. We grab a bandage, an ice pack, or call for help if it's serious. A first aid kit brings comfort and protection. Jesus is like the greatest Rescuer of all time.

Jesus didn't come to earth to judge us or point out everything we do wrong. He came because He loves us too much to leave us hurting and far from God. Every person has sins—mistakes, wrong choices, and things that damage our hearts. Jesus came to rescue us from those things and to heal us from the inside out.

As we begin the season of Easter, we remember that Jesus' mission was love , to bring us close to God and give us new life. We can celebrate that Jesus came not to condemn but to save and restore.

Jesus is our hope, our rescuer, and our forever friend.

Family Discussion Questions

1. Why is it important that Jesus came to save and not condemn?
2. What are ways Jesus has helped heal our hearts?
3. How can we share Jesus' love with others this week?

Prayer

Jesus, thank You for coming to save us. Thank You for loving us even when we mess up. Help us remember that Your love brings healing and hope to the whole world. Amen.

Family Challenge of the Week

As a family, look for one person to show "rescue" love to. Someone who needs help, encouragement, or kindness this week.

Devotional 2
THE CROSS & GOD'S GREAT LOVE

Verse of the Week

This is how God showed his love among us: He sent his one and only Son into the world that we might live through him. This is love: not that we loved God, but that he loved us and sent his Son as an atoning sacrifice for our sins.
-1 John 4:9–10(NIV)

Object Lesson

Take a piece of paper and write a few simple "wrongs" kids can relate to (arguing, not listening, being unkind). Then draw a big cross over the whole page so the words are covered.

Devotional

Sometimes we wonder how much God really loves us. The cross gives us the answer.

God saw the sin in our hearts, the things that separate us from Him, but He didn't turn away. Instead, He chose to do something about it. Jesus came and took every single sin with Him to the cross. He traded our brokenness for His forgiveness. He showed us what real love looks like: love that sacrifices, love that forgives, love that chooses us even when we don't deserve it.

When Jesus died on the cross, it wasn't the end — it was the greatest rescue plan ever completed. The cross shows us that God's love is bigger than our mistakes, stronger than our fears, and deeper than we can imagine.

Every time you see a cross, remember: *"God loves me so much that He gave everything to bring me close to Him."*

Family Discussion Questions

1. What do you think of when you see a cross?
2. How does it feel knowing Jesus chose to take away our sins?
3. How can we show others sacrificial love like Jesus?

Prayer

Lord, thank You for the cross. Thank You for loving us so much that You sent Jesus to save us. Help our hearts stay full of gratitude for Your great love. Amen.

Family Challenge of the Week

Make a "Cross of Love."

Make a cross to display somewhere visible this week. Decorate it together. Use it as a reminder to show extraordinary love.

Devotional 3
THE EMPTY TOMB: HOPE LIVES!

Verse of the Week

Praise be to the God and Father of our Lord Jesus Christ! In his great mercy he has given us new birth into a living hope through the resurrection of Jesus Christ from the dead, and into an inheritance that can never perish, spoil or fade.
-1 Peter 1:3–4(NIV)

Object Lesson

Show an empty Easter egg. Ask: *"Is it disappointing when something is empty?"* Then explain that one empty place changed everything — Jesus' tomb.

Devotional

Most of the time, empty things feel disappointing — an empty snack bag, an empty toy shelf, or an empty battery. But the empty tomb is completely different!

After Jesus died, His friends thought the story was over. They were sad, scared, and confused. But on the third day, something miraculous happened... Jesus rose from the dead! When they found His tomb empty, everything changed. Empty meant victory. Empty meant hope. Empty meant *Jesus is alive*!

Because Jesus conquered death, we can have hope even on our hardest days. Hope that God is working. Hope that nothing is too big for Him. Hope that Jesus gives us new life forever.

The empty tomb reminds us that when things look impossible, God can still bring joy, life, and miracles.

Family Discussion Questions

1. Why did the empty tomb give Jesus' friends hope?
2. How does Jesus being alive affect our lives today?
3. Where do you need God's hope right now?

Prayer

Jesus, thank You for the empty tomb and the hope it gives us. Help us remember that You are alive and always with us. Fill our hearts with joy today. Amen.

Family Challenge of the Week

Celebrate hope! Choose one way to spread joy. Write encouraging notes, brighten someone's day with a surprise, or pray together for someone who needs hope.

Devotional 4
LIVING AS FOLLOWERS OF JESUS

Verse of the Week

"A new command I give you: Love one another. As I have loved you, so you must love one another. By this everyone will know that you are my disciples, if you love one another." -John 13:34–35(NIV)

Object Lesson

Hold up a jersey or team shirt. Explain that teams are recognized by what they wear, but Christians are recognized by how they love.

Devotional

Every team has a way to show who they belong to with a logo, color, or mascot. Jesus said His followers would be known not by what they wear, but by something far more important: their love.

When Jesus rose from the dead, He didn't just want His disciples to *remember* what He did — He wanted them *to live it out*. Loving others the way Jesus loves us means being kind, patient, forgiving, and willing to help everyone, not just the people we like.

We shine Jesus' love when we treat others the way He would. Every time we choose love instead of anger, patience instead of frustration, or forgiveness instead of holding a grudge, the world sees Jesus in us.

Let our home, our school, and our community know who we belong to, because our love looks like Jesus.

Family Discussion Questions

1. What are some ways people can tell we follow Jesus?
2. When is it hardest to love others like Jesus?
3. What is one way our family can show Jesus' love this week?

Prayer

Jesus, thank You for showing us how to love. Help our family be known for kindness, patience, and compassion. Let others see You through the way we treat them. Amen.

Family Challenge of the Week

Become "**Team Jesus.**"

Pick one loving action to do together. Visit someone, help a neighbor, or choose a random act of kindness as "Team Jesus" this week.

MAY

GRATITUDE & JOY

Devotional 1
THANKING GOD IN ALL THINGS

Verse of the Week

Rejoice always, pray continually, give thanks in all circumstances; for this is God's will for you in Christ Jesus.
-1 Thessalonians 5:16–18(NIV)

Object Lesson

Place two jars on the table: one labeled "Complaints" and one labeled "Thanks." Give everyone slips of paper and have them write down one of each. Notice which jar fills faster and how giving thanks feels different.

Devotional

It's easy to give thanks when good things happen: sunny days, yummy snacks, fun plans. But what about when days are boring, someone hurts our feelings, or plans change? The Bible encourages us to give thanks in *all* circumstances, not because every moment is fun, but because God is always with us.

Being thankful changes our hearts. It reminds us of what God is doing, even when we can't see it yet. Gratitude gives us joy, even in tough moments, because we remember we're never alone.

God isn't asking us to pretend bad things don't happen. He's asking us to trust Him through everything. When we choose thankfulness, we shift our focus from what is wrong... to the One who makes all things right.

Family Discussion Questions

1. When is it hardest for you to give thanks?
2. What are three things you can thank God for today?
3. How does being thankful change the way you feel?

Prayer

God, help us rejoice always, pray continually, and give thanks in every situation. Open our eyes to see Your goodness all around us. Amen.

Family Challenge of the Week

Start a "**Family Gratitude Jar.**"

Every day this week, each person writes down one thing on a slip of paper they're thankful for. Add it to the jar. At the end of the week, read them together as a family.

Devotional 2
JOY IN THE EVERYDAY

Verse of the Week

This is the day that the Lord has made; let us rejoice and be glad in it. -Psalm 118:24(ESV)

Object Lesson

Set a timer for 15 seconds and have everyone find something in the room that brings them joy. Share what you found and why.

Devotional

Some days feel exciting: birthdays, vacations, surprises. Those are easy "rejoice" days! But most days are simple and ordinary. Wake up, school or work, meals, chores, sleep. Psalm 118 reminds us: every day is a gift from God.

Joy isn't something we wait for, it's something we choose. God made today on purpose, and there is joy hidden everywhere: in laughter at the dinner table, in the beauty of nature, in the people we love, and in the little blessings we might overlook.

When we wake up and say, *"Thank You, God, for THIS day,"* it changes how we see the hours ahead. Joy shows up in the ordinary when our hearts are looking for it. Even a day that feels "boring" can become full of wonder when we remember God is with us.

We don't have to wait for the weekend or a special event to celebrate the goodness of God. We can look for His fingerprints in tiny moments like a hug, a cozy blanket, a delicious snack, or a moment of peace after a busy afternoon.

Choosing joy helps us see that God is caring for us every single day. When we decide to rejoice today, we are saying, *"God, I trust You. I'm glad to be alive, and I'm grateful for what You've given."*

Family Discussion Questions

1. What was one joyful moment from today?
2. How can we look for joy even on boring or tough days?
3. What does it mean that God made "this day" for us?

Prayer

Lord, thank You for today! Fill our hearts with joy and help us notice Your blessings in big and small ways. We choose to rejoice because You are good. Amen.

Family Challenge of the Week

Declare one day this week "**Joy Day.**"

Look for moments of happiness and write them down or take photos to remember them.

Devotional 3
A HEART OF CELEBRATION

Verse of the Week

Shout for joy to the Lord, all the earth. Worship the Lord with gladness; come before him with joyful songs. Know that the Lord is God. It is he who made us, and we are his; we are his people, the sheep of his pasture. Enter his gates with thanksgiving and his courts with praise; give thanks to him and praise his name. For the Lord is good and his love endures forever; his faithfulness continues through all generations. -Psalm 100:1–5(NIV)

Object Lesson

Play a worship song and have a mini family praise party with singing, dancing, instruments, clapping. Anything that celebrates God joyfully!

Devotional

God loves celebration! Psalm 100 says to shout for joy, worship with gladness, and come before Him with singing. Why? Because God is good and His love never ends.

Celebration isn't just for holidays. It's a way of remembering how amazing God is. When we celebrate Him, our hearts fill with joy, and we grow closer to Him. Celebration reminds us that God is powerful, loving, and always with us. Even when we're facing challenges, praise helps us remember that God is bigger and stronger than anything we face.

A heart of celebration doesn't depend on perfect circumstances, it depends on a perfect God. When we celebrate who He is, joy flows out and spreads to others.

Family Discussion Questions

1. What is one thing about God you want to celebrate today?
2. How does worship help us feel closer to God?
3. How can we make celebration a regular part of our home?

Prayer

God, we celebrate Your goodness and everlasting love! Fill our home with praise and joy. Help us worship You with our whole hearts. Amen.

Family Challenge of the Week

Choose a time this weekend to have a **Family Praise Celebration**. Play worship music, pray together, and celebrate God's goodness!

Devotional 4
GOD'S GOOD GIFTS

Verse of the Week

Every good and perfect gift is from above, coming down from the Father of the heavenly lights, who does not change like shifting shadows. -James 1:17(NIV)

Object Lesson

Give everyone a sticky note and have them label different "gifts" from God around the house (family, food, books, pets, sunshine, etc.).

Devotional

Every good thing we enjoy comes from God, not just big gifts like birthdays and vacations, but the everyday blessings we might forget: a warm bed, clean water, hugs, laughter, music, and friends. Sometimes we think of gifts as things wrapped in shiny paper or surprises that suddenly appear. But God's gifts are wrapped in ordinary moments, they are everywhere! When we pause to notice them, it feels like discovering hidden treasures in our day.

Recognizing God's generosity fills our hearts with thankfulness and reminds us that we are deeply loved. He isn't stingy or distant, He is constantly pouring out kindness, hoping we'll notice and celebrate His goodness. Even on hard days, God still gives us good gifts such as hope, peace, comfort, and His presence. When we learn to see God as the Giver of all good things, our hearts fill with gratitude and joy, and we begin to see that every day with Him is a gift worth celebrating.

Family Discussion Questions

1. What is one "good gift" from God you noticed today?
2. How does it feel knowing God wants to bless us?
3. How can we use God's gifts to bless others?

Prayer

Thank You, God, for every good gift You give us. Help us notice Your blessings and use them to show love to others. Thank You for being a generous Father. Amen.

Family Challenge of the Week

Be a blessing.

Choose one "good gift" your family has: time, a talent, or belongings, and use it to bless someone else this week.

JUNE

STRENGTH IN GOD

Devotional 1
GOD IS OUR PROTECTOR

Verse of the Week

So do not fear, for I am with you; do not be dismayed, for I am your God. I will strengthen you and help you; I will uphold you with my righteous right hand.
-Isaiah 41:10(NIV)

Object Lesson

Have a parent stand behind a child as they gently lean back into their arms. A trust fall. Explain: *"You were confident to lean back because you trusted I would catch you."*

Devotional

There are times when we feel worried, scared, or unsure of what will happen next. God knows those moments can make our hearts shake. That's why He promises to be with us, not from far away, but right beside us, ready to catch us when we feel like we're falling.

Isaiah 41:10 reminds us that God doesn't want fear to control our lives. He is our protector and our strength. When we feel weak, He lifts us up. When we don't know what to do, He guides us. When we feel alone, He reminds us that His hand is holding us tight.

God doesn't promise that scary things will never happen, but He does promise that **we will never face them alone**. We can trust Him because He loves us and He is stronger than anything we will ever face.

Family Discussion Questions

1. What is something that makes you feel afraid or unsure?
2. How does knowing God is with you help you feel braver?
3. What does it look like to "lean on" God in real life?

Prayer

God, thank You for being our protector. When we are scared, help us remember that You are holding us and giving us strength. Amen.

Family Challenge of the Week

Create a "**Courage List**."

Each family member writes down 1 thing they want to trust God with this week. Hang the list somewhere you'll see it daily. Pray over those challenges each night and celebrate even the smallest steps of courage God helps you take.

Devotional 2
STANDING STRONG IN HARD TIMES

Verse of the Week

Even though I walk through the valley of the shadow of death, I will fear no evil, for you are with me; your rod and your staff, they comfort me. -Psalm 23:4(ESV)

Object Lesson

Dim the lights or step into a dark hallway. Explain how darkness can feel scary, but holding someone's hand immediately helps us feel safe. We don't have to see everything clearly to know someone we trust is with us.

Devotional

Life isn't always bright and easy. Sometimes we go through "dark valleys" or moments when we feel sad, worried, or confused. David, who wrote Psalm 23, understood this. He knew that even when life is scary, God walks right beside us.

Strength doesn't mean we never feel afraid. It means that even when fear tries to control us, we remember Who is with us. God is our shepherd, leading us through every challenge and lighting the way.

There will be days when friends are hurtful, school is tough, or we feel lonely. But God promises that we never have to walk through those moments by ourselves. He gives us the strength to keep moving, even when things feel dark.

Jesus is our comfort, our guide, and our constant helper. Always close, always loving.

Family Discussion Questions

1. What are some "dark valley" moments kids or adults may face?
2. How has God brought you through something difficult before?
3. What does it mean to trust God even when life feels scary?

Prayer

Lord, thank You for staying close in our hardest moments. Help us remember that You are our shepherd, leading us through every dark valley. Amen.

Family Challenge of the Week

Encourage someone going through a tough time. Send a card, make a drawing, or say a prayer together for them. A small act of kindness can remind them they're not alone and that God cares about what they're facing.

Devotional 3
COURAGE TO DO WHAT'S RIGHT

Verse of the Week

Who is going to harm you if you are eager to do good? But even if you should suffer for what is right, you are blessed. "Do not fear their threats; do not be frightened." But in your hearts revere Christ as Lord. Always be prepared to give an answer to everyone who asks you to give the reason for the hope that you have. But do this with gentleness and respect. -1 Peter 3:13–15(NIV)

Object Lesson

Give two choices written on cards: one easy but unkind, one kind but brave. Talk about why the right choice can sometimes be the harder one.

Devotional

Doing what's right isn't always simple. Sometimes being kind, honest, or standing up for someone comes with challenges. Maybe it feels awkward or we worry about what others will think.

But God gives us courage to stand strong. Courage isn't about being the biggest or the boldest, it's about trusting God when the right choice feels difficult. 1 Peter reminds us that when we choose to do what is good and right, God is with us. We don't have to be afraid of others' opinions because our strength comes from Him.
Jesus always chose love, even when it meant sacrifice.

When we follow His example by helping someone, telling the truth, including someone lonely — we show the world what God's love looks like.

Courage comes from knowing God is on our side, helping us take the right step every time.

Family Discussion Questions

1. When have you had to make a brave choice to do what's right?
2. Why does doing the right thing sometimes feel hard?
3. How can we encourage each other to be courageous?

Prayer

God, give us courage to do what is right, even when it's difficult. Help us shine Your love wherever we go. Amen.

Family Challenge of the Week

Each person chooses one courageous act of kindness to do this week: at school, at home, or in the community. Write it down and pray that God will help you be brave enough to follow through. Big or small, courage makes a difference!

Devotional 4
GOD HELPS US HELP OTHERS

Verse of the Week

For I was hungry and you gave me food, I was thirsty and you gave me drink, I was a stranger and you welcomed me, I was naked and you clothed me, I was sick and you visited me, I was in prison and you came to me.' Then the righteous will answer him, saying, 'Lord, when did we see you hungry and feed you, or thirsty and give you drink? And when did we see you a stranger and welcome you, or naked and clothe you? And when did we see you sick or in prison and visit you?' And the King will answer them, 'Truly, I say to you, as you did it to one of the least of these my brothers, you did it to me.' -Matthew 25:35–40(ESV)

Object Lesson

Set a table with items for a meal. Talk about ways your family has helped others (food drives, donations, checking on neighbors) and how those actions show God's love.

Devotional

Helping others isn't just a nice thing to do, it's one of the ways we show Jesus how much we love Him. In Matthew 25, Jesus tells us that whenever we feed someone who is hungry, welcome someone who feels left out, or care for someone in need... **we are actually serving Him.**

God gives us strength not just for ourselves, but so we can use it to make a difference in someone else's life. When we help, encourage, or support others, we are spreading God's love into the world.

No act of kindness is too small. God sees every caring moment and uses it to show people His heart. We never know how much hope our kindness can bring to someone who is hurting.

Jesus said, *"What you did for the least of these, you did for Me."* That means every time we serve someone, we are serving Jesus.

Family Discussion Questions

1. Who in our life might need help or encouragement right now?
2. What are some small ways we can serve others this week?
3. How does it feel to know we are serving Jesus when we help others?

Prayer

Jesus, thank You for giving us the strength to help others. Open our eyes to see who needs love and give us willing hearts to serve like You. Amen.

Family Challenge of the Week

Choose one way to serve together as a family this week: deliver a meal, donate items, or help a neighbor with a chore.

JULY

FREEDOM IN CHRIST

Devotional 1
WHAT TRUE FREEDOM MEANS

Verse of the Week

To the Jews who had believed him, Jesus said, "If you hold to my teaching, you are really my disciples. Then you will know the truth, and the truth will set you free."
-John 8:31–32(NIV)

Object Lesson

Tie a loose scarf or string around someone's wrists. Ask them to pretend they're "stuck" and try to move freely. Then remove the string and show how much easier it is to move when nothing holds you back.

Devotional

We often think of freedom as simply doing whatever we want. But Jesus teaches a different kind of freedom, one that starts in our hearts. When we follow His teachings, we learn what is true and good, and that truth sets us free from the things that weigh us down.

Sin, fear, lies, and bad choices can make us feel "stuck." They trap our hearts and make us feel less like who God created us to be. But Jesus came to break those chains! When we follow Him, we don't have to live trapped anymore.

Jesus doesn't just set us free from something, He sets us free for something: a life filled with purpose, joy, and peace. True freedom is found in living the way Jesus designed us to live — close to Him, confident in His love, and unafraid of anything holding us back.

Family Discussion Questions

1. What are some things that might make people feel "stuck" inside?
2. How does Jesus help us live free?
3. What does it mean to follow Jesus' teachings?

Prayer

Jesus, thank You for giving us true freedom. Help us hold tightly to Your truth so we can live the full, joyful life You have for us. Amen.

Family Challenge of the Week

Write "**FREEDOM IN JESUS**" on a poster.

Each day, add one thing Jesus has freed you from or one blessing His freedom brings. Let this become a visual reminder that His grace gives us a fresh start every day.

Devotional 2
LETTING GO OF SIN & SHAME

Verse of the Week

Therefore, there is now no condemnation for those who are in Christ Jesus, because through Christ Jesus the law of the Spirit who gives life has set you free from the law of sin and death. -Romans 8:1–2(NIV)

Object Lesson

Give each family member a heavy book (or other item) to hold. Talk about how long they could carry it before it becomes tiring. Then set the books down and notice the relief of letting go.

Devotional

Sin and shame can feel like heavy weights we drag around. Mistakes we wish we could erase, moments we feel guilty, or times we think, "I'm not good enough." But God never intended us to carry those burdens forever.

Jesus came to set us free from sin's grip and the shame that follows. When we confess our sin, He doesn't hold it against us, He forgives completely. Romans 8 reminds us that once we belong to Jesus, there is no condemnation, meaning God isn't pointing a finger at us saying "You're guilty." Instead, He says, "You're forgiven. You're free."

Letting go of shame means trusting that Jesus' sacrifice is enough. We don't have to stay stuck in yesterday's mistakes. He gives us a new start — and a lighter, freer heart.

Family Discussion Questions

1. Why do you think shame feels so heavy?
2. How does Jesus help us let go of past mistakes?
3. What does God want us to remember when we mess up?

Prayer

Jesus, thank You for taking away our sin and shame. Help us live in Your freedom and remember that we are loved and forgiven. Amen.

Family Challenge of the Week

Let go.

Write a mistake or worry on a piece of paper. Pray together, then tear it up or throw it away. Reminding yourselves that Jesus sets us free!

Devotional 3
FREE TO SERVE

Verse of the Week

You, my brothers and sisters, were called to be free. But do not use your freedom to indulge the flesh; rather, serve one another humbly in love. -Galatians 5:13(NIV)

Object Lesson

Give each person a paper crown and celebrate your "freedom." Then turn the crowns into serving hats (or aprons) to show that real freedom loves to help others.

Devotional

When Jesus frees us, it's not so we can live selfishly. Freedom isn't a license to do whatever we want, it's power to do what God wants! And one of God's favorite things is when we serve others with love.

Serving doesn't make us weaker, it shows real strength. Jesus, the King of Kings, washed His friends' feet to teach us that greatness comes from helping others, not from being first or getting our own way.

We are most free when we love like Jesus. Putting others first, noticing needs, and being willing to help even when it costs us something. Serving turns our freedom into a blessing for the world.

Family Discussion Questions

1. What is the difference between selfish freedom and serving freedom?
2. Who is someone you can serve this week?
3. How does serving others show the love of Jesus?

Prayer

Lord, thank You for the freedom we have in You. Help us use our freedom to love and serve others. Make our hearts more like Yours. Amen.

Family Challenge of the Week

Choose one service activity to do together. Help a neighbor, volunteer, or make a kindness card for someone who needs encouragement.

Devotional 4
CHOOSING GOD'S WAY

Verse of the Week

For all that is in the world—the desires of the flesh and the desires of the eyes and pride of life—is not from the Father but is from the world. And the world is passing away along with its desires, but whoever does the will of God abides forever. -1 John 2:16–17(ESV)

Object Lesson

Place two paths on the floor using masking tape. One shorter and easy, the other longer with twists and obstacles. Place a covered treat at the end of the hard one. Place something icky, covered at the end of the easy one. Let kids walk both and talk about how and why the easy path isn't always the best one.

Devotional

Every day we make choices — what we say, how we treat others, who we listen to, and what we believe. Some choices are easy but lead us away from God's best. Others are harder but lead to real life and joy.

The world tells us, "Do what feels good" or "Make yourself happy first." But God's way is different. He invites us to follow Him, even when it means taking the harder path. Because His way leads to blessings that last forever.

Choosing God's way means trusting that His plans are

better than anything the world offers. It means saying "yes" to what is right, loving, and true, even when it's not popular. With Jesus, we have the freedom to walk a new path, one filled with hope, joy, and purpose.

Family Discussion Questions

1. What are some examples of "easy" choices that aren't the best?
2. How does God help us choose His way?
3. What's a decision you can make this week that honors God?

Prayer

God, help us choose Your way every day. Give us wisdom to make good choices and courage to follow You. Thank You for the freedom to live for You. Amen.

Family Challenge of the Week

Pick one goal as a family. Like praying together or showing kindness daily and follow God's way together all week.

AUGUST

WISDOM & CHOICES

Devotional 1
ASKING GOD FOR WISDOM

Verse of the Week

If any of you lacks wisdom, you should ask God, who gives generously to all without finding fault, and it will be given to you. -James 1:5(NIV)

Object Lesson

Place several puzzle pieces on the table. Ask one family member to assemble them without seeing the box cover. After they struggle for a bit, show the full picture. The puzzle becomes easier when they know what they're making!

Devotional

Life is full of decisions — what to say, how to act, who to spend time with. Some choices are small, like what to wear or what snack to eat, but others feel big and overwhelming. Sometimes it feels like we're trying to solve a giant puzzle without knowing what the final picture is supposed to look like. That's why God invites us to ask Him for wisdom! He wants to help us every step of the way.

God sees the whole picture of our lives. The past, present, and future, even when we can only see one moment at a time. When we don't know what to do, we can pause and pray, *"God, please show me the wise choice."* He speaks through His Word, through godly advice, and through the peace He places in our hearts. Wisdom doesn't mean always picking what's easiest or most fun, but choosing what is right in God's eyes.

The best part? God never gets tired of helping us. He loves when we come to Him with our questions and decisions. When we trust Him to guide us, we become stronger, kinder, and more like Jesus. Wisdom grows little by little as we **practice listening to God, one choice at a time!**

Family Discussion Questions

1. When was a time you needed wisdom?
2. What's the difference between knowledge and wisdom?
3. How can we remember to ask God before making decisions?

Prayer

God, thank You for knowing the full picture of our lives. Help us remember to ask You for wisdom every day. Show us Your path and help us walk in it. Amen.

Family Challenge of the Week

Create a "**Wisdom Prayer.**"

As a family, create a "Wisdom Prayer" card to keep by the door or on the fridge. Pray it every morning before starting your day or when you are unsure of what to do.

Devotional 2
MAKING WISE DECISIONS

Verse of the Week

Your word is a lamp for my feet, a light on my path.
-Psalm 119:105(NIV)

Object Lesson

Turn off the lights and try walking across a room. Then turn on a flashlight and do it again. Which was easier?

Devotional

Have you ever tried walking in the dark? It feels uncomfortable, confusing, and even a little scary. That's exactly how life can feel when we try to make choices without God's guidance.

But God hasn't left us to stumble around blindly! He gave us His Word—**the Bible**—as a bright flashlight to light up our hearts and show us the way. When we open Scripture, we find clear direction about what is right, what pleases God, and what blesses the people around us.

Some decisions are small, like what to eat or which game to play, while others are much bigger. Like how to forgive someone who hurt us, how to stand up for truth, or who to let close as friends. God promises that when we look to His Word first, He will always shine enough light for the very next step, even if we can't see the whole path yet.

Family Discussion Questions

1. Can you think of a Bible verse that has helped you make a good decision?
2. What "big" choices might we face this week?
3. How can we use God's Word like a light in those moments?

Prayer

Lord, thank You for the Bible and the way You guide us through it. Help us turn to Your Word whenever we feel unsure. Light up our path so that we walk with wisdom. Amen.

Family Challenge of the Week

Choose one Bible verse about wisdom and memorize it together. Say it each night before bed.

Devotional 3
SURROUND YOURSELF WITH GOOD FRIENDS

Verse of the Week

And let us consider how to stir up one another to love and good works, not neglecting to meet together, as is the habit of some, but encouraging one another, and all the more as you see the Day drawing near. -Hebrews 10:24-25(ESV)

Object Lesson

Place two plants side by side. One healthy and one droopy. Talk about how the healthy plant might need extra sun and water, while the weak one needs support to stand tall. Good friends help each other grow!

Devotional

Friends make everything more exciting. Laughing together, playing games, going on adventures, and making memories that last. But the people we hang out with also shape who we become. The Bible says good friends help us do what's right, cheer us on, and keep pointing us to Jesus.

Sadly, some friends can pull us toward meanness, trouble, or habits that hurt us. That's why choosing our friends carefully is one of the biggest decisions we'll ever make. God wants us to pick friends who build others up, who choose kindness, and who help us love Him more.
He also calls us to be that kind of friend ourselves. When we surround ourselves with people who love God and love others, our faith grows stronger every single day.

Family Discussion Questions

1. What qualities make someone a good friend?
2. How can *you* encourage a friend to make good choices?
3. Do you feel like you are a "builder-upper" friend?

Prayer

Father, thank You for the friends in our lives. Help us choose friends who encourage us, and help us be friends who show Your love every day. Amen.

Family Challenge of the Week

Do one kind thing for a friend this week to help build them up. A note, a treat, a prayer, or an invitation to play.

Devotional 4
WHEN YOU MAKE MISTAKES

Verse of the Week

If we say we have no sin, we deceive ourselves, and the truth is not in us. If we confess our sins, he is faithful and just to forgive us our sins and to cleanse us from all unrighteousness. -1 John 1:8–9(ESV)

Object Lesson

Take a whiteboard and write a few "mistakes" in marker (or use a piece of paper with a pencil and eraser). Then erase them completely. God wipes our hearts clean when we confess our sins!

Devotional

Everyone makes mistakes—parents, kids, teachers, pastors, literally every person on earth. We say hurtful words we wish we could unsay, we choose wrong even when we know better, and sometimes we hurt the people we care about. Those moments can leave us feeling embarrassed, ashamed, guilty, or even afraid of what others will think. But God never wants us to stay trapped in that heaviness.

Instead, He opens His arms and invites us to come straight to Him, tell Him exactly what we did wrong, and ask for forgiveness. When we confess, God doesn't yell, shame us, or keep a record of our wrongs, *He completely wipes them away*. His love covers everything and gives us a brand-new start, every single time we need it.

Making mistakes is part of growing, and learning from them helps us become wiser and stronger. Your failures do not get the final say about who you are... **Jesus does**. He looks at you and says, *"Forgiven, loved, and mine."* That's your true identity, now and forever.

Family Discussion Questions

1. What should we do when we realize we've done something wrong?
2. How does it feel to know God always forgives us?
3. How can we show forgiveness to others like Jesus does for us?

Prayer

God, thank You for loving us even when we make mistakes. Help us come to You quickly with honest hearts and help us offer forgiveness to others. Thank You for fresh starts. Amen.

Family Challenge of the Week

If someone in your family gets upset or makes a mistake, practice saying: *"I forgive you. Let's try again."* Offer grace freely!

SEPTEMBER

SERVING OTHERS

Devotional 1
SEEING PEOPLE THE WAY GOD DOES

Verse of the Week

Dear friends, since God so loved us, we also ought to love one another. No one has ever seen God; but if we love one another, God lives in us and his love is made complete in us. -1 John 4:11–12(NIV)

Object Lesson

Place a pair of sunglasses or glasses on the table. Try them on one by one. Some might be dark, some bright, some funny. Explain that the way we "see" people can change based on what "lens" we use. God wants us to see others through *His lens* of love.

Devotional

Sometimes we only notice what makes people different. Their accent, their clothes, the things they like, or how they act. It's easy to stop there and judge or pull away. But God never does that. He looks past the outside and sees straight into every person's heart.

Every single person you meet, at school, in the store, or even in your own family, *is deeply loved by God*. He made them on purpose and calls them priceless. When we start seeing people the way God sees them, everything about how we treat them changes.

Instead of judging, *we listen*; instead of ignoring, *we care*;

instead of teasing, *we choose kindness*. When we love others like this, God's own love shines through us like light through a window.

We become little mirrors that reflect His heart to the world. That's the beautiful way people around us get to meet the real God—through the love we show them every day.

Family Discussion Questions

1. What does it mean to "see others like God sees them"?
2. Who is someone you can show God's love to this week?
3. What helps us remember that every person is valuable to God?

Prayer

God, thank You for loving every person so much. Help us look at others through Your eyes. With love, compassion, and kindness. Show us how to reflect Your love to others this week. Amen.

Family Challenge of the Week

Practice seeing others with love by giving **three genuine compliments** to different people this week.

Devotional 2
HELPING AT HOME

Verse of the Week

He must manage his own family well and see that his children obey him, and he must do so in a manner worthy of full respect. If anyone does not know how to manage his own family, how can he take care of God's church? -1 Timothy 3:4–5(NIV)

Object Lesson

Give everyone a small puzzle piece or block. One person tries to build something on their own. It falls apart or doesn't look right. Then everyone works together. It becomes strong and beautiful. Homes grow stronger when everyone helps!

Devotional

Serving others doesn't have to be a giant thing; some of the best ways to serve start right in your own house. Making your bed, clearing the table, helping a brother or sister, or folding laundry might look small, but each one is a real way to say "*I love you*" without words. When everyone pitches in, home feels happier, calmer, and full of peace.

God smiles when families work together because home is the very first place He teaches us how to love like Jesus. Jesus didn't come to be waited on, He came to serve everyone around Him. Every time we choose to help instead of walking away, encourage instead of grumbling, or jump in before anyone asks, we look a little more like Him.

Serving at home isn't just another chore; it's a gift we give and receive. It fills our hearts and the hearts of the people we love with real joy that only comes from loving like Jesus does.

Family Discussion Questions

1. What is one thing you can do every day to help at home?
2. How does it feel when someone serves you out of love?
3. How can helping become a joyful part of our day?

Prayer

Jesus, thank You for our family and our home. Help us look for ways to serve each other with happy hearts. Teach us to follow Your example of love through our actions. Amen.

Family Challenge of the Week

Create a "**Serve at Home**" bingo card.

Add chores or acts of kindness to help eachother. Try to fill the whole card together!

Devotional 3
SERVING IN YOUR COMMUNITY

Verse of the Week

Love the Lord your God with all your heart and with all your soul and with all your mind and with all your strength.' The second is this: 'Love your neighbor as yourself.' There is no commandment greater than these." -Mark 12:30-31(NIV)

Object Lesson

Fill two cups. One overflowing with water, one nearly empty. Which cup can give more? When our hearts are filled with God's love, we have more to pour into others!

Devotional

Our community is so much bigger than just the people inside our house—it includes neighbors, classmates, teachers, coaches, and even the cashier at the store. Jesus tells us to love every one of them the same way we love ourselves. That kind of love isn't far away or fancy; it happens right where we are every day.

Serving our community can be super simple: holding a door, picking up trash at the park, praying quietly for a neighbor, or writing a quick thank-you note to a teacher. None of these things take much time, but each one carries Jesus' kindness into someone else's day.

We never know how big a tiny act can feel to the person who receives it. A smile might chase away loneliness, a helping hand might remind someone they're not forgotten. When we love and serve the people around us, we become part of what God is doing in our neighborhood. Through our small choices, others get to meet Jesus, and our whole community starts looking a little more like His love!

Family Discussion Questions

1. Who in our community could use encouragement right now?
2. What is a simple way we can serve someone outside our home this week?
3. Why do you think Jesus cares so much about us loving our neighbors?

Prayer

Lord, thank You for placing us in this community. Open our eyes so we can notice people who need love and help us serve them with joyful hearts. Use us to show Your kindness wherever we go. Amen.

Family Challenge of the Week

Choose one **community service activity** to do together. Food pantry volunteer night, cards or artwork for nursing homes/hospitals, donate & deliver pet supplies to an animal shelter, or make blessing bags for the homeless shelters.

Devotional 4
SHARING YOUR FAITH

Verse of the Week

... Always be prepared to give an answer to everyone who asks you to give the reason for the hope that you have. ...
-1 Peter 3:15(NIV)

Object Lesson

Give each person a flashlight. Have them shine their lights in different directions. Talk about how each beam goes into dark places. Just like our faith can shine into someone's life!

Devotional

If you discovered the most incredible treasure in the whole world, would you hide it away or shout it from the rooftops so everyone could find it too? Knowing Jesus is exactly that kind of treasure. The very best gift anyone could ever receive. His love changes everything about our lives, from the inside out.

When we talk about Jesus, we're simply passing that treasure along to others. You don't need to be a preacher or memorize the whole Bible to do it. All you have to do is share what He's done for you. How He fills your heart with peace, how He forgives every mistake, and how He helps you love people in ways you never could before.

Sharing your faith can be as easy as inviting a friend to church with you, offering to pray for someone who's hurting, or telling a quick story about how God helped you through a tough day. Even the smallest light can brighten a dark room. When we let our little light shine, God uses it to guide others straight to His love!

Family Discussion Questions

1. What do you love most about Jesus?
2. Who is someone you can share your faith with this week?
3. What are some simple ways to shine your light?

Prayer

Jesus, thank You for giving us a hope we can share. Make us brave and loving as we shine Your light into the lives of others. Help people see You when they see us. Amen.

Family Challenge of the Week

Be a "prayer warrior."

Each family member chooses one person to pray for every day, asking God for a chance to show or share His love.

OCTOBER

LIGHT IN THE DARKNESS

Devotional 1
JESUS IS THE LIGHT

Verse of the Week

When Jesus spoke again to the people, he said, "I am the light of the world. Whoever follows me will never walk in darkness, but will have the light of life." -John 8:12(NIV)

Object Lesson

Turn off all the lights in a room. Try walking around. Then turn on one lamp or flashlight. Notice how even a small light changes everything. Bringing clarity, comfort, and safety.

Devotional

Darkness can feel really scary. It's hard to see where you're going, and you might bump into things or feel totally lost. Jesus says that without Him, our hearts can feel just like that. Confused, afraid, and unsure which way is right.

But Jesus didn't come to leave us stumbling around in the dark. He came to be the *bright light that shines right into our lives*. When we follow Him, He shows us what is good, what is true, and how to love the way He loves.

His light chases away sadness with hope and gives us courage when we're afraid. No darkness, no matter how big, whether it's confusion, fear, or wrong choices, is ever stronger than Jesus' light. **When He is near, darkness never wins**; He always lights the next step forward!

Family Discussion Questions

1. What are some "dark" things in the world that Jesus' light can overcome?
2. When have you felt Jesus helping you in a difficult or scary moment?
3. How can we stay close to His light every day?

Prayer

Jesus, thank You for being the light of the world and the light in our hearts. Help us follow You closely so we never walk in darkness. Shine bright through us. Amen.

Family Challenge of the Week

Do some **star gazing**.

Spend one evening outside looking at stars. Talk about how Jesus' light is even brighter and never goes out. (Best to go to a dark park outside of the city)

Devotional 2
BEING A LIGHT AT SCHOOL & HOME

Verse of the Week

Neither do people light a lamp and put it under a bowl. Instead they put it on its stand, and it gives light to everyone in the house. In the same way, let your light shine before others, that they may see your good deeds and glorify your Father in heaven. -Matthew 5:15-16(NIV)

Object Lesson

Give each family member a small glass jar and a battery tea light. When everyone turns on their light and places them together, the glow becomes brighter. Just like how our lights shine stronger when we shine together!

Devotional

Think about the kindest person you know. The friend who always makes room for someone new, the teacher who notices when you're quiet and sad, or the sibling who helps without being asked. Their little acts of kindness make the whole day better for everyone around them. That's exactly the way Jesus wants us to shine every single day.

You don't need a microphone or a big stage to show Jesus to the world. You shine right where you are—at the lunch table, on the playground, while doing chores, or just talking with friends. When people see love, joy, honesty, and patience coming from you, they're actually getting a glimpse of Jesus Himself.

Your light might feel tiny sometimes, like a single candle in a big room, but God loves to use even the smallest glow to warm someone's heart and brighten their whole day. Yes, shining can feel hard when everyone else is acting grumpy or selfish, but keep going anyway. God promises that when we choose kindness for Him, people will notice His goodness and feel His love through us!

Family Discussion Questions

1. What is one way you can shine Jesus' light at school tomorrow?
2. Who needs encouragement at home or school?
3. How does shining our light bring glory to God?

Prayer

Lord, help our light shine brightly everywhere we go. Make our actions show others Your love in real and powerful ways. Amen.

Family Challenge of the Week

Choose one "**light action**" to do at school or home each day. Such as encouraging a classmate, letting someone go first, or helping with chores before being asked.

Devotional 3
WHEN LIFE FEELS SCARY

Verse of the Week

God is our refuge and strength, an ever-present help in trouble. Therefore we will not fear... -Psalm 46:1-2(NIV)

Object Lesson

Give everyone a balloon and have them slowly blow into it while thinking of something that causes fear or worry. Then, let the air out together. Reminding one another that we can "*let go*" of our fear because God is with us.

Devotional

There are moments when fear feels huge, like a thunderstorm shaking the windows, a really hard test, a big change, or that empty feeling when you think you're all alone. In those times, your heart starts racing and your mind fills with the scariest "what-ifs." Fear tries to shout louder than everything else.

But God has a stronger voice, and He says something amazing: "*I am with you—always.*" He never walks away when life gets scary; He stays closer than your own heartbeat. He is your safe shelter, your strong house, and your strength when your legs feel wobbly.

The world might look dark and uncertain, but God's light never flickers out. Even when you can't see the path ahead, He is already there, walking right beside you and guarding you every step. When worry knocks, you can breathe deep and whisper, *"God, You are here. I don't have to be afraid."* His perfect love wins over fear, every single time!

Family Discussion Questions

1. What is something that scares you or makes you feel worried?
2. How can remembering God's presence help during those moments?
3. What Bible verses comfort you when you're afraid?

Prayer

God, thank You for being our strong protector. When we feel afraid, remind us that You are right beside us. Help us trust You with our whole hearts. Amen.

Family Challenge of the Week

Make "**God's Got It**" jar.

Write down fears on slips of paper and place them in a jar labeled "God's Got It." Pray over them together this week.

Devotional 4
SHINING GOD'S LIGHT THROUGH KINDNESS

Verse of the Week

Follow God's example, therefore, as dearly loved children and walk in the way of love, just as Christ loved us and gave himself up for us as a fragrant offering and sacrifice to God.
-Ephesians 5:1–2(NIV)

Object Lesson

Take a plain piece of paper and cut out a star. Then decorate it with markers or glitter. Explain that kindness makes us "shine" brighter. Every act of kindness adds another sparkle to our light!

Devotional

Jesus didn't just talk about love, He lived it out in every moment. He fed crowds of hungry people, sat with those who were hurting and felt forgotten, and welcomed the ones everyone else turned away from. When we choose kindness like that, we're following right in Jesus' footsteps, letting His light spill out into our everyday world.

Kindness has real power. It can turn someone's whole day around or even change the course of their life forever. You never know how far a single kind act might ripple, touching hearts you can't even see. A simple smile can warm up a lonely heart; a gentle word can calm a brewing argument; a helping hand can spark courage in someone who feels stuck.

Being kind is one of the brightest, most beautiful ways we show Jesus to the people around us. And here's the best part: the more kindness you pour out, the more your own heart glows with God's endless love. It's like a chain reaction... *your light makes everyone brighter!*

Family Discussion Questions

1. What are some simple ways to show kindness every day?
2. Why do you think kindness is such a powerful way to share God's love?
3. Who can you show kindness to this week?

Prayer

Jesus, help us follow Your example of love. Fill our hearts with kindness so Your light can shine through us everywhere we go. Amen.

Family Challenge of the Week

Be a *Mission Fat Hearts* Secret Agent.

Do a **secret kindness mission** for someone. Leave a note, help with a chore, or share something special — without expecting thanks.

(Visit our website MissionFatHearts.com to learn more.)

NOVEMBER

THANKFULNESS & CONTENTMENT

Devotional 1
GRATITUDE EVEN WHEN IT'S HARD

Verse of the Week

Give thanks in all circumstances; for this is God's will for you in Christ Jesus. -1 Thessalonians 5:18(NIV)

Object Lesson

Place two jars on the table: one labeled "Blessings" and one labeled "Complaints." Throughout the day, have the family try to fill the "Blessings" jar faster. At the end of the day, count what you wrote.

Devotional

It's super easy to say "thank you" when life feels perfect.On bright sunny days, having exciting plans, eating delicious food, and saying prayers that get a quick yes. But what about the days that feel heavy, stressful, or just plain disappointing? The Bible asks us to give thanks in every single circumstance, even the tough ones.

Why would God ask that? Because He never stops being good, even when everything else feels bad. In the middle of hard moments, He is still working behind the scenes, holding us close, and loving us perfectly. Thankfulness doesn't mean pretending the hard stuff isn't real; it means remembering that God is bigger than the hard stuff and always with us.

When we choose to look for even tiny blessings during

challenges, our hearts grow stronger and hope starts pushing worry away. Gratitude opens our eyes to God's gentle fingerprints all over our ordinary days. Every time we say thank you, whether with a smile or through tears, we're really telling God, "*I trust You*," and that makes our faith shine even brighter!

Family Discussion Questions

1. What is something hard you can thank God for this week?
2. How can gratitude change the way we feel about our day?
3. What are three blessings you're thankful for today?

Prayer

Lord, thank You for being good all the time, even when life feels hard. Teach us to look for Your blessings and to trust that You are always with us. Amen.

Family Challenge of the Week

Have each person choose one **"hard thing"** happening right now and write down three reasons to thank God in the midst of it.

Devotional 2
BEING CONTENT WITH WHAT WE HAVE

Verse of the Week

I know what it is to be in need, and I know what it is to have plenty. I have learned the secret of being content in any and every situation, whether well fed or hungry, whether living in plenty or in want. -Philippians 4:12(NIV)

Object Lesson

Lay out several wrapped boxes — some fancy, some plain. Explain that contentment isn't about the "package," but the heart inside. What matters most isn't what we have, but Who we have in our lives.

Devotional

We live in a world that never stops whispering, "You need more!" More toys, cooler clothes, the newest gadget, bigger adventures. It feels like everyone is racing to grab the next thing, and if we don't keep up, we'll miss out. But chasing "more" is like trying to fill a bucket with a hole in it. Our hearts never feel full.

God wants us to discover the secret the apostle Paul learned: contentment. Contentment is being truly thankful and happy with what God has already placed in our hands. When we keep our eyes on Jesus, His never-ending love, His always-there presence, and every good gift He's given, **peace settles deep inside us.**

Contentment doesn't mean we stop dreaming or working toward goals. It just means we refuse to let those wants steal our joy today. Whether we have a little or a lot, *Jesus is always enough*. When we rest in that truth, we find the kind of happiness no amount of stuff can ever buy!

Family Discussion Questions

1. What is something you're tempted to think you "need" to be happy?
2. How can we practice contentment every day?
3. Why is Jesus enough for us?

Prayer

God, help us be content with the blessings You've already given us. Teach us to find joy in You rather than in things. Fill our hearts with peace and thankfulness. Amen.

Family Challenge of the Week

Operation "**Give away.**"

Go through your toys or belongings together. Choose items in good condition to give away to a church pantry or homeless shelter.

Devotional 3
THANKING GOD FOR PEOPLE

Verse of the Week

I always thank my God for you because of his grace given you in Christ Jesus. -1 Corinthians 1:4(NIV)

Object Lesson

Pass around a mirror. Each person looks into it, then says: "*I am someone God made on purpose and someone others can thank God for.*" Celebrate each person's uniqueness!

Devotional

People are one of the very best gifts God ever gives us. Our families who hug us when we're sad, friends who make us laugh, teachers who believe in us, leaders who guide us, and neighbors who wave hello. God hand-picked every one of them to love us, cheer us on, and help us grow. Yet we often remember to thank God for toys, food, or sunny days, but forget to thank Him for the hearts beating right next to ours.

The apostle Paul never forgot. In almost every letter he wrote to churches, he started by thanking God for the people there. He knew how much relationships matter to God's heart. When we tell someone "*I'm so thankful for you,*" it's like giving them a warm blanket for their soul.
A simple thank-you can remind them that God sees them, loves them, and thinks they're priceless.

Today, let's celebrate the people who make our lives brighter and richer. Look them in the eyes, send a note, or give a hug, and say the words out loud: "*I thank God for you!*" That little moment of gratitude builds stronger friendships and shows everyone around us how big God's love really is.

Family Discussion Questions

1. Who is someone you are especially thankful for this week?
2. What makes the people in your life special?
3. How can you show gratitude to someone today?

Prayer

God, help us be content with the blessings You've already given us. Teach us to find joy in You rather than in things. Fill our hearts with peace and thankfulness. Amen.

Family Challenge of the Week

Write thank-you notes (or draw pictures) for three people you appreciate and deliver them!

Devotional 4
LIVING A LIFE OF PRAISE

Verse of the Week

In him we were also chosen, having been predestined according to the plan of him who works out everything in conformity with the purpose of his will, in order that we, who were the first to put our hope in Christ, might be for the praise of his glory. -Ephesians 1:11–12(NIV)

Object Lesson

Give each family member a sticky note and ask them to write or draw one thing God has done. Stick them all on a wall to create a big "praise collage" of God's goodness!

Devotional

Praise isn't only singing beautiful worship songs at church, though that's one of the sweetest ways to lift our hearts to God. Real praise is a whole-life thing; it's letting everything we do, say, and think point back to how amazing He is. It looks like choosing gratitude when we feel like complaining, picking joy when grumbling feels easier, and loving others even when we're tired.

When we live like that, people around us notice something different, something brighter, and that brightness is *God's glory shining through us*. Praise turns regular moments, washing dishes, walking to school, or helping a friend, into little acts of worship. Even a quiet whisper of *"Thank You, God"* makes heaven smile.

We were made on purpose to show the world how good God is. Every time we choose to praise, our hearts snuggle closer to His. No matter what kind of day we're having, God is always worthy of our praise, *always*!

Family Discussion Questions

1. What are some ways we can praise God outside of church?
2. How does praise change the attitude of our hearts?
3. What's one moment this week when you saw God's goodness?

Prayer

Lord, You deserve all our praise. Help our words and actions reflect Your love and goodness. Fill our hearts with joy every day as we thank You for who You are. Amen.

Family Challenge of the Week

Have a **Praise Party Night**!

Play worship music, share blessings from the week, and celebrate God's goodness together.

DECEMBER

JESUS: GOD'S GREATEST GIFT

Devotional 1
THE PROMISE OF A SAVIOR

Verse of the Week

For to us a child is born, to us a son is given, and the government will be on his shoulders. And he will be called Wonderful Counselor, Mighty God, Everlasting Father, Prince of Peace. Of the greatness of his government and peace there will be no end. He will reign on David's throne and over his kingdom, establishing and upholding it with justice and righteousness from that time on and forever. The zeal of the Lord Almighty will accomplish this.
-Isaiah 9:6–7(NIV)

Object Lesson

Wrap a small gift box and place it somewhere visible. Tell your kids that they can't open it until the end of the week. Talk about how waiting for something special can be hard, but it's worth it!

Devotional

Long before Jesus was born, God made a promise. Through the prophet Isaiah, He told the world that a Savior was coming. Someone who would bring hope, peace, joy, and love. People waited a **long time** for that promise to come true, but God never forgot. He was carefully preparing the perfect moment for Jesus to enter the world.
Sometimes we feel like we wait a long time for things, too. For a prayer to be answered, for healing, or for something exciting to happen. But just like God kept His promise of

sending Jesus, we can *trust Him* to keep His promises today. Every time we celebrate Christmas, we are celebrating a God who shows up right on time.

As we wait for Christmas morning, let's remember that Jesus is the greatest gift the world has ever received, a Savior who came to rescue us and show us God's unending love.

Family Discussion Questions

1. Why do you think God made a promise long before Jesus was born?
2. What is something you are waiting on God for right now?
3. How does it help to remember that God keeps His promises?

Prayer

Dear God, thank You for promising Jesus long ago and for always keeping Your promises. Help us trust You when we have to wait. Amen.

Family Challenge of the Week

Make a "**Promise Box.**"
Write promises of God from the Bible on slips of paper and read one each day.

Devotional 2
THE BIRTH OF JESUS

Verse of the Week

And there were shepherds living out in the fields nearby, keeping watch over their flocks at night. An angel of the Lord appeared to them, and the glory of the Lord shone around them, and they were terrified. But the angel said to them, "Do not be afraid. I bring you good news that will cause great joy for all the people. Today in the town of David a Savior has been born to you; he is the Messiah, the Lord. -Luke 2:8–11(NIV)

Object Lesson

Turn off the lights and use a flashlight. Shine it around the room, then read Luke 2:10–11. Talk about how the good news of Jesus was like a light breaking into the darkness.

Devotional

The night Jesus was born was a quiet night, just like many others before it. But suddenly, the sky lit up with God's glory, and shepherds heard the most exciting news ever: *"A Savior has been born to you!"*

Jesus didn't arrive in a castle or with a royal parade. He came as a tiny baby, born in a stable, laid in a manger. God sent His Son in the most humble way, showing us that His love is for *everyone*. No one is too small, too plain, or too unimportant for God's attention.

Christmas is so much more than presents, cookies, and decorations — **it's about celebrating the moment God came near**. Emmanuel, God with us. The manger reminds us that Jesus came to rescue us and to live with us forever.

Let the lights, the songs, and the celebrations this month remind you that the Light of the World has come!

Family Discussion Questions

1. Why do you think God chose shepherds to hear the good news first?
2. What does it mean that God is "with us"?
3. How can our family celebrate Jesus more this Christmas?

Prayer

Jesus, thank You for coming into our world to save us. Help us remember that You are the reason we celebrate Christmas. Amen.

Family Challenge of the Week

Bake cookies or treats for someone who may feel alone this Christmas. A neighbor, a church member, a friend, or a nursing home.

Devotional 3
GIVING LIKE JESUS GAVE

Verse of the Week

In everything I did, I showed you that by this kind of hard work we must help the weak, remembering the words the Lord Jesus himself said: 'It is more blessed to give than to receive.' " -Acts 20:35(NIV)

Object Lesson

Wrap up something that belongs to you (a toy, book, or craft) and give it away to someone who will enjoy it. Talk about how giving something you love shows real generosity.

Devotional

Jesus didn't come to earth to *get* things. He came to **give**. He gave His time, His love, His kindness, and ultimately His life — all because He loves us so much. And the Bible says, "It is more blessed to give than to receive." That means giving brings more joy than getting!

This time of year, it's easy to focus on wish lists and gifts we want. But when we give, especially when it costs us something, we become more like Jesus. It could be offering help, giving a hug, sharing a favorite toy, or simply choosing kind words. Every act of giving shines His love into the world.

What if this Christmas, instead of thinking *"What will I get?"*, we prayed, "*God, who can I bless today?*"

Jesus showed us that the true joy of Christmas comes from loving others well.

Family Discussion Questions

1. What is something you could give that would bless someone else?
2. How does giving make you feel?
3. Why do you think Jesus loved to serve and give?

Prayer

Lord, help us be generous like Jesus. Show us who needs love and help us give joyfully. Amen.

Family Challenge of the Week

Choose one toy, book, or item each family member can donate to someone in need.

Devotional 4
PEACE ON EARTH & IN OUR HEARTS

Verse of the Week

Peace I leave with you; my peace I give you. I do not give to you as the world gives. Do not let your hearts be troubled and do not be afraid. -John 14:27(NIV)

Object Lesson

Take a snow globe and shake it. Watch the pieces swirl, then slowly settle. Explain that sometimes our hearts feel chaotic like that, but Jesus brings peace that calms us.

Devotional

Life can feel busy, noisy, and even a little stressful, especially at Christmas. But Jesus came to bring peace. Not just peace on earth, but peace *inside* our hearts. When the angels announced Jesus' birth, they declared "peace on earth" because the Savior had come. The One who would restore our relationship with God.

Peace doesn't mean everything around us is perfect. It means that even when things feel crazy, when plans change, when someone is upset, when we feel worried, we can rest in God's love. Jesus is like the calm in the middle of our snow-globe moments.

Whenever you feel anxious, take a deep breath and remember: **Jesus is with you**. He offers a peace that the world can't give, a peace that reminds us we are safe in His hands.

Family Discussion Questions

1. What makes you feel stressed or worried sometimes?
2. How can we ask Jesus for peace when life feels busy?
3. How can our family bring peace to others this week?

Prayer

Jesus, thank You for being our Prince of Peace. Help calm our hearts when we feel worried and help us share Your peace with others. Amen.

Family Challenge of the Week

Create a **"peace corner"** at home. A quiet spot where anyone can go to pray, breathe, and find calm.

FINAL THOUGHTS

Congratulations, amazing family! You did it! You made it through an entire year of seeking Jesus together, and that is worth celebrating with the biggest high-fives, happy dances, and maybe even extra ice cream!

Growing closer to Christ side-by-side is one of the most beautiful adventures you will ever share. The laughs around the table, the quiet prayers at bedtime, the questions you wrestled with together, and the verses you now know by heart—*every single moment mattered*. God has been weaving your family tighter together and closer to His heart all year long.

So don't stop here! Keep carving out that special time each week. Whether it's Sunday breakfast devotions, Wednesday night Bible-and-pajamas time, or a quick verse and prayer in the car. Keep reading Scripture out loud, keep asking big questions, keep sharing highs and lows, and keep cheering each other on to love Jesus more. Some weeks will feel easy and sweet, others might feel busy or messy, but every time you open God's Word together, He promises to show up.

You've already built something priceless: **a family that runs to God together**. Keep growing, keep learning, keep laughing, keep praying, and keep trusting that the same God who carried you this far will lead you into even more joy in the years ahead. The best is still to come because you're doing this with Jesus!

EXTRAS

Family Faith Milestones Tracker

This year, your family will grow in so many beautiful ways, not just in knowledge, but in trust, courage, love, and everyday faith. Use this page to mark the special spiritual moments that happen along the way.

You can write the date, a short note, or even add a picture or a drawing!

Milestone	Date
We completed our first devotional together	
Someone prayed out loud for the first time	
A memory verse became a family favorite	
We served someone outside our family	
We invited a friend to church	
God answered a big prayer	
We made a faith decision (baptism, salvation, recommitment)	

Add more rows as your family continues to grow!

You'll be amazed looking back at all God has done.

What we want to remember

Monthly Memory Verse Review

Each month has one key verse that reminds your family of the theme God is teaching. Use this section to celebrate progress, practice verses, and reflect on what God is showing your family.

You can check off when each verse is memorized, write how God used that verse in your week, or jot down a simple prayer of thanks.

Month	Memory Verse
January	2 Corinthians 5:17
February	John 3:16
March	Luke 8:11, 15
April	John 3:17
May	1 Thessalonians 5:16–18
June	Isaiah 41:10
July	John 8:31–32
August	James 1:5
September	1 John 4:11–12
October	John 8:12
November	1 Thessalonians 5:18
December	Isaiah 9:6–7

Tip: Celebrate each verse learned with a family treat or a happy dance!

Memorized?	Notes

Notes & Reflections Pages

As you journey through the year, God may whisper something special into your hearts. This space is for capturing those moments...

• Something God showed us this week
• A prayer we want to keep praying
• A verse that felt extra important
• Questions we want to ask later
• A story from our family challenge
• A praise report of what God has done

You can doodle, write bullet points, or fill the page with colorful drawings — whatever helps your family remember God's goodness.

Notes & Reflections Pages

Faith isn't just something we read — it's something we live. These pages are here to help your family look back and see a whole year filled with God's love, kindness, and faithfulness.

Notes & Reflections Pages

Notes & Reflections Pages

Notes & Reflections Pages

Notes & Reflections Pages

About the Author

Rebecca graduated from Malone College in 2008 with a Bachelor's degree in Youth Ministry. She started writing & illustrating in 2013, about her dog Pookie, when she wanted a fun and wholesome story for her nieces and nephews, some of which were learning to read. She plans to keep up her series and write others. In 2019, she launched a publishing and entertainment company to help kids explore and nurture their creative side through books, tv shows, and art classes.

Along with *The Adventures of Pookie* children's book series, she is the illustrator of her sister, Megan Yee's books in the God's Books series. She is also the author of the personal development book *The Creative Minds Guide to Success*. She travels full time in a 5th wheel RV with her husband Eric, and their dog, Bailey, for his job as a Journeyman Lineman and writes about their adventures along the way.

The Adventures of
Pookie
ENTERTAINMENT

Books   Shows   Classes

Check out more:

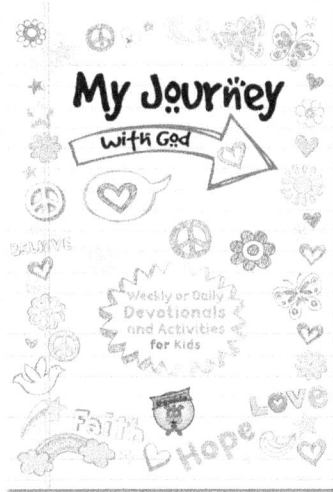

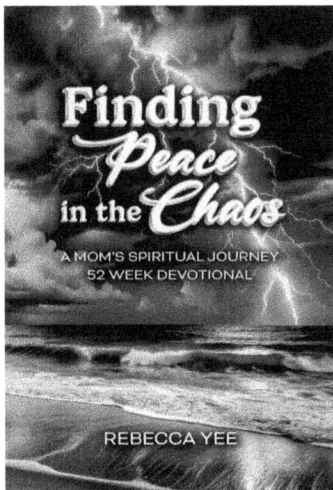

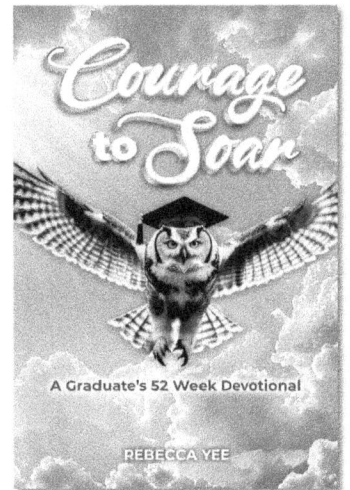

God's Masterpiece

My Journey with God
Weekly or Daily Devotionals and Activities for Kids
Faith • Hope • Love

God's Little Pumpkin
Megan Yee   Rebecca Yee

God's Snowman
Written By Megan Yee   Illustrated By Rebecca Yee

Love, Jesus
Written by Megan Yee   Illustrated by Rebecca Yee

52 WEEK DEVOTIONAL FOR THE HEART OF A FATHER
STRENGTH To Lead
REBECCA YEE

Finding Peace in the Chaos
A MOM'S SPIRITUAL JOURNEY 52 WEEK DEVOTIONAL
REBECCA YEE

Courage to Soar
A Graduate's 52 Week Devotional
REBECCA YEE

AdventuresOfPookie.com